The Bizarre History of Beauty

SCARY SKIN CARE

ANITA CROY

Gareth Stevens
PUBLISHING

Please visit our website, www.garethstevens.com.
For a free color catalog of all our high-quality books,
call toll free 1-800-542-2595 or fax 1-877-542-2596.

Cataloging-in-Publication Data
Names: Croy, Anita.
Title: Scary skin care / Anita Croy.
Description: New York : Gareth Stevens Publishing, 2019. | Series: The bizarre history of beauty | Includes
glossary and index.
Identifiers: ISBN 9781538226865 (pbk.) | ISBN 9781538226858 (library bound)
Subjects: LCSH: Skin–Care and hygiene–Juvenile literature. | Beauty, Personal–Juvenile literature.
Classification: LCC RL87.C79 2019 | DDC 646.7'2–dc23

First Edition

Published in 2019 by
Gareth Stevens Publishing
111 East 14th Street, Suite 349
New York, NY 10003

Produced for Gareth Stevens by Calcium
Editors: Sarah Eason and Tim Cooke
Designers: Clare Webber and Lynne Lennon
Picture researcher: Rachel Blount

Picture credits: Cover: Shutterstock: Lucky Business; Inside: Shutterstock: Alfernec: p. 39t; CSMaster:
p. 12b; Demisteriman: p. 11t; DenisProduction.com: p. 43t; Everett Collection: p. 37; Everett Historical:
p. 5b; Featureflash Photo Agency: p. 43b; Fotos593: p. 6; Funtap: p. 25t; Keith Homan: p. 5t; Jstone:
p. 41; Unchalee Khun: p. 12t; Dorothea Lange: p. 38; Lestertair: p. 4; Sergey Lukyanov: p. 11b; Makistock:
p. 40; Moravska: p. 15b; Nattanan726: p. 9t; Angela N Perryman: p. 16; Smarina: p. 39b; Christopher
Sprake: p. 29; Toong Stockers: p. 23t; Swapan Photography: p. 17t; Varuna: pp. 1, 42; Wikimedia
Commons: pp. 10, 13, 23b, 35b; John Bell: p. 27; Henry Pierce Bone: p. 24; Art by Henry Cline,
lithograph by the Morgan Litho. Co., Cleveland, Ohio: p. 33b; FA2010: p. 35t; Martin Le France: p. 19;
formerly attributed to Marcus Gheeraerts the Younger, exhibited 2003 as British School: p. 20; James
Holland, RWS: p. 26; Internet Archive Book Images: p. 33t; Jllm06: p. 32; B.J. Johnson Soap Company,
Inc.: p. 30; Leyo: p. 21; After Rowland Lockley: p. 18; Master of the Coronation of the Virgin: p. 15t;
National Photo Company: p. 31; Marie-Lan Nguyen/collection of Giampietro Campana di Cavelli; 1861:
purchased: p. 9b; Carole Raddato: p. 7; Joshua Reynolds: p. 22; Touriste: p. 17b; U.S. National Archives
and Records Administration: p. 36; Henry Wallis: p. 25b; Wellcome Images: pp. 8, 28; Rogier van der
Weyden: p. 14; Eartha M.M. White Collection: p. 34.

Printed in the United States of America

CPSIA compliance information: Batch #CS18GS:
For further information contact Gareth Stevens, New York, New York at 1-800-542-2595.

-CONTENTS-

Chapter 1

THE ANCIENT
- WORLD -

In the ancient world, the softness of your skin said a lot about you. Only the poor and those who had to work outside had rough or burned skin. That meant most people.

Ancient civilizations looked to nature for skin-care products. The earliest **hunter-gatherers** smeared mud or berry juice on their bodies to protect their skin or to keep themselves hidden when they were hunting. They soon learned that some substances made their skin feel better.

NATURE'S BOUNTY

Many of the ancient peoples based in what are now Egypt and the Middle East had easy access to useful herbs and **minerals**. The Hebrews crushed tree bark to make oils that helped clean the skin and keep it free of rashes and infections. The ancient Egyptians took skin care to a new level. They used honey, milk, and herbs to keep their skin soft.

Mud baths were popular from early in human history. Mud contains minerals that soften and **rejuvenate** the skin.

Keeping the skin soft was just part of life. The Egyptians also used creams to avoid wrinkles, which made them look old. Important Egyptians were buried with anti-wrinkle creams so they could use them in the **afterlife**.

EARLY POTIONS

As long ago as AD 200, the Greek physician Galen made the first face cream. He mixed **rosewater**, beeswax, and olive oil to make a **cold cream** to remove dirt, oil, and dead cells from the skin. Other ancient civilizations used foods to treat the skin. The Romans mixed wine with milk and bread to make a paste they wore as a **face mask**. Many other foods were used in a similar way, including ground corn, powdered eggshells, ground almonds, and poppy seeds. Most of these were harmless, but ancient peoples also used lead-based products to soften their faces. They did not realize that lead facemasks were potentially deadly and dangerous.

Mr. Theron Pond of New York invented a modern cold cream in 1846. This was over 1,600 years after Galen.

Galen (right) was renowned as a physician. His cures were used for centuries.

EGYPTIAN
- SKIN CARE -

The ancient Egyptians knew a lot about taking care of themselves. Skin care was a major pastime for wealthy men and women.

The Egyptians were not particularly choosy about what they put on their faces. As long as it made their skin clear and shiny, they were happy to give it a try.

DO YOU EAT IT?

One recipe for getting rid of bad skin was a face mask using a mixture of bull's bile, olive oil, whipped ostrich eggs, dough, and milk. These were mixed with natron, a natural salt found in dried lake beds, and sticky **resin** from trees. To get rid of wrinkles and keep their skin smooth, Egyptians mixed together scented gum, olive oil, crushed cyperus (a type of grass), and wax. They smeared the mixture on their faces and left it there for six days. It may have been effective, but they must have smelled quite bad!

Natron and resin must have been effective potions—the Egyptians also used them to preserve dead bodies as **mummies**.

MILK AND OILS

Although it was easier for wealthy people to keep their skin clean and smooth, all ancient Egyptians believed that cleanliness was important. Nearly everyone bathed twice a day. In the first century BC, Queen Cleopatra kept 700 donkeys to provide milk for baths to keep her skin soft. About 2,000 years later, scientists figured out that special acids in milk act as **exfoliators** and skin softeners, and milk was reintroduced as a beauty treatment. The Egyptians had as many as 30 different **moisturizers** made from animal fat, plant oils, flowers, and herbs, such as thyme, frankincense, and myrrh. Perfumed oils were handed out to workers and farmers with their food. The wealthy moisturized using a cream made from a fruit named quince and rinsed the face with refreshing rosewater.

As well as bathing in milk, Cleopatra probably used egg whites to clean and soften her face, as did many other wealthy Egyptians.

to die for

Some Egyptian beauty practices were painful. To get rid of body hair, people used light pumice stones to rub it away from the skin! The Egyptians thought that varicose veins on the legs were attractive, so they highlighted them with blue paint. These swollen veins hurt a lot, however. Today, doctors get rid of them.

LOTIONS AND
- POTIONS -

The Egyptians were not the only ancient people to care about their skin. The Mesopotamians of modern-day Iraq and the ancient Greeks and Romans all had their own ideas about beauty.

The Greeks liked to keep their bodies smelling clean—even when they were dirty. As early as the ninth century BC, women sprinkled runners and wrestlers at sports tournaments with perfume to take away the smell of sweaty bodies. Boys held trays with herbs and spices, and each victor was given a crown of sweet-smelling frankincense.

KEEPING CLEAN

The Romans conquered Greece in the second century BC and Egypt a century later. They kept themselves very clean—even without soap. The Romans went to public baths where they rubbed their bodies with olive oil and then got hot and sweaty. They scraped off the dirt that came out of their skin with a curved implement called a strigil.

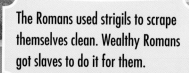

The Romans used strigils to scrape themselves clean. Wealthy Romans got slaves to do it for them.

I DON'T THINK SO!

In Rome, a pale **complexion** was all the rage. Romans made face packs from barley flour and butter and protected their skin with oils made from herbs and almonds. They also used face packs made from mud. Mud had been used for a similar purpose for centuries by peoples living along rivers or on lakes. The mud contained minerals that helped nourish the skin. Peoples across North Africa often used it to cover their bodies and faces. To give their nails a pink glow, the Romans painted them with a mixture of sheep fat and blood.

The first century AD poet Ovid had a hot tip for keeping a smooth complexion: a face pack of crocodile excrement!

hello beautiful

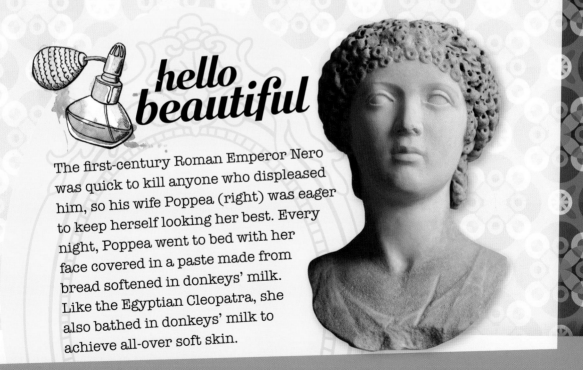

The first-century Roman Emperor Nero was quick to kill anyone who displeased him, so his wife Poppea (right) was eager to keep herself looking her best. Every night, Poppea went to bed with her face covered in a paste made from bread softened in donkeys' milk. Like the Egyptian Cleopatra, she also bathed in donkeys' milk to achieve all-over soft skin.

Chapter 2
THE MIDDLE
- AGES -

The Roman Empire was overthrown by Germanic peoples in AD 57. Trade in the former empire suffered, and so did the cleanliness of the inhabitants.

The Romans had believed in keeping clean and smelling good. They saw their public bathhouses as a symbol of a modern society. But in the Middle Ages, the baths were seen as a sign of an **immoral** empire that deserved to fall.

GOD'S GIFTS

Christianity was the dominant force in medieval Europe. Christian teaching urged people to accept their place in life and personal qualities as gifts from God—even if that meant a bad complexion or strong body odor. Trying to improve their appearance with skin care suggested that someone was not grateful to God. As a result, most Christians smelled bad and didn't look much better.

An apothecary or druggist teaches his helper about his different potions.

BEAUTY OR MEDICINE?

Later in the Middle Ages, attitudes began to change. Druggists called apothecaries opened stores in towns and cities to sell herbs and ready-mixed potions. Most of their preparations were used to treat medical problems. However, some of them were also useful for treating zits or other beauty problems. It was just important not to admit the real reason you wanted them, or people might think you were being **vain**, which was seen as a sin. None of these medieval remedies were for the faint-hearted. Apothecaries' preparations were based on homeopathy, or treating a condition with something related to it. A tonic called the King's Drops, which was used to treat headaches, was made from powdered skull mixed with alcohol! Other common products found at apothecaries' stores included animal excrement and urine.

There was a trend for white skin—a sign that women did not have to work outdoors. Some women used **leeches** to suck their blood to make their faces look paler. Leeches were regularly used to remove blood from people with a range of diseases.

The English king Charles II was said to have invented the King's Drops.

Physicians used leeches when they thought a patient's blood was poisoned and had to be removed.

SKIN
- CARE -

In the early Middle Ages, virtually anything could be used on the skin. Some of the ingredients were expensive and others were strange, but they seem to have worked.

To try to achieve the desirable unmarked, smooth skin of a woman of leisure, women used face creams made from animal fat, starch, and tin. Another common ingredient was the slime from snails. The slime stimulated the skin to produce natural chemicals that keep the skin soft and supple. Snail slime is still used in face creams today.

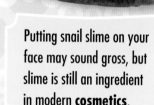

Putting snail slime on your face may sound gross, but slime is still an ingredient in modern **cosmetics**.

WHAT'S IN THE JAR?

Every woman's dread was pimples. If a zit broke out, women turned to **gemstones** to help. The most valued zit-buster was the purple amethyst crystal, which was rubbed directly over the pimple to get rid of it. Other ingredients women used on their faces included aloe vera, vinegar, strawberry juice, and the sheep's rampion plant. Another way to keep skin smooth and pale was to drink the sap of the willow tree, which was extracted from the bark by boiling it in water.

Amethyst was used as a charm by the ancient Greeks.

WHAT ABOUT THE MEN?

While women did their best to look pale and smooth, most European men were still hairy and smelly. One notable exception was the Vikings from Scandinavia. These farmers and seafarers began to raid parts of Europe from around the ninth century onward. The Vikings had a bad reputation among other Europeans because they were not Christians, but they were some of the cleanest people in the medieval world. They bathed at least once a week and used strong soap. They even had tiny spoons to pull wax out of their ears. The Anglo-Saxons of England, in contrast, bathed once a year. What was more, Viking men were partial to a bit of **kohl** around the eyes to give them a tough look. Unlike women, it did not matter if men had dark, tanned skin, as they were outdoors most of the time.

hello beautiful

When Isabeau of Bavaria married King Charles VI of France in 1385, she became queen of France. She did not have the pale look so prized in the medieval world— but she did have lots of money to take care of herself. She bathed in donkeys' milk and slathered her face with a lotion made from boars' brains, crocodile glands, and wolves' blood to keep her looking young.

Isabeau (center) arrives at church for her wedding.

IT'S NOT
-FAIR-

The desired look for a medieval lady was fair, pale, and smooth-skinned. Sadly, other looks risked being seen as the work of the devil.

The main beauty feature was a high forehead, which women achieved by pushing back their hair and shaving off their eyebrows. That left them with an awful lot of exposed skin. For the effect to work, that skin had to be flawless.

KEEP IT SMOOTH

No one wanted any imperfections: no freckles, pimples, or moles. A mark on the face was seen as a stain of the devil. It could get a woman excluded from society. That put a lot of pressure on the daily beauty routine. Popular face masks to deliver smooth, blemish-free skin included a mixture of oatmeal boiled with vinegar. Some women also tried smearing their face with a mask of bull's or hare's blood.

Medieval women displayed so much forehead that they were eager to make sure their skin was as clear as it could be.

PALE AND INTERESTING

Just as the ancient Egyptians had used blue paint to highlight varicose veins in their legs, medieval women highlighted the veins on their chests. They painted the veins blue to provide a contrast that made their skin appear even paler and more **translucent**—and therefore a little more fashionable. Skin had to be hairless as well as pale. One way of getting rid of unwanted hair was to make a paste of red orpiment (a mineral), ivy, ants' eggs, and vinegar. The paste was smeared over the unwanted hair to make it fall out.

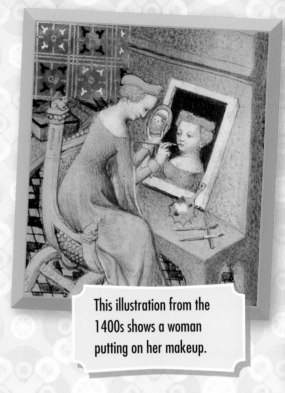

This illustration from the 1400s shows a woman putting on her makeup.

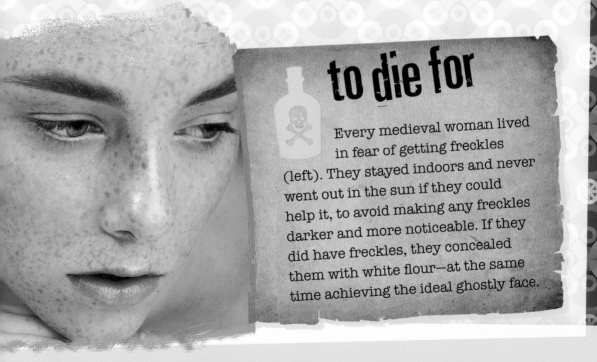

to die for

Every medieval woman lived in fear of getting freckles (left). They stayed indoors and never went out in the sun if they could help it, to avoid making any freckles darker and more noticeable. If they did have freckles, they concealed them with white flour—at the same time achieving the ideal ghostly face.

HOME FROM
- THE CRUSADES -

Between the eleventh and thirteenth centuries, European Christians and Muslims fought a long series of crusades, or holy wars, in the Holy Land in the Middle East.

In 1095, Pope Urban II called on all Christians to free the holy places in the Holy Land from Muslim control. Many knights went to fight. In return, Urban promised that their sins would be forgiven.

THAT'S NEW

After 200 years, the Crusades ultimately failed to take control of the holy sites. However, they changed the face of Europe—and of Europeans! The men who went off to the Middle East were bearded and usually smelly. The men who came home were clean-shaven and smelled good. The Crusades also opened new trade routes that allowed Europeans to buy spices, herbs, and minerals for cosmetics, such as **alum**, frankincense, and myrrh.

The new trade routes to Asia gave Europeans access to a range of spices that helped their skin— and made food taste better!

EXOTIC TREATMENTS

Many of these new imports were not that new. The Romans had started using them after they conquered present-day Turkey in 129 BC. Alum was an **astringent**, so it got rid of pesky pimples and blemishes. Frankincense and myrrh, which was made from the stem of a bushy shrub, were great moisturizers, as were walnut bark and anise. The Crusaders were surprised to find that people in the Middle East had good teeth. The Muslims chewed walnut bark to keep their gums healthy and fiber from tree roots that acted as toothbrushes. However, all these products had to be imported long distances from the Middle East to parts of Europe. That made them rare and expensive.

Frankincense was an aromatic oil made from the sap of tea trees.

hello *beautiful*

The most famous beauty of the twelfth century was Eleanor of Aquitaine, who was queen of both France and England. Despite having 10 children, she still had time for her beauty regime. Contemporaries said she was "more than beautiful" well into her old age.

Eleanor of Aquitaine (left) married King Louis VII of France and then King Henry II of England (right).

Chapter 3

THE EARLY
-MODERN AGE-

At the end of the Middle Ages, keeping clean and using makeup came back into fashion. Now, the more cosmetics, the better. Looking ugly could cost someone their life!

Renaissance artists and thinkers wanted to return to the classical ideas of ancient Greece and Rome. They thought a lot about the nature of beauty.

ALL CHANGE

Italy was the heart of the Renaissance, and the Italian city of Venice set the trends for beauty. The Venetians were first to receive the new herbs and spices arriving from Asia and soon tried them as cosmetics. Meanwhile, in Florence, Agnolo Firenzuola published one of the first beauty books, *On the Beauty of Women*.

Mary Queen of Scots was said to keep her skin looking youthful by bathing in wine made from berries of the elder bush.

BY ROYAL COMMAND

As always, royalty was in the forefront of fashion. In Italy, Catherine de Medici swore by pigeon dung to keep her complexion looking young. In France, Diane de Poitiers had more expensive taste. She drank liquid gold to keep herself looking young. The Tudors in England with their "scrubbed faces" lagged behind the made-up Europeans. That changed in January 1559, when Elizabeth I became queen of England and the most powerful woman in Europe. All women wanted to copy Elizabeth's pale ivory complexion and red hair. They might not have been as eager to try the urine Elizabeth wiped on her teeth in order to whiten them. Wealthy men and women also used puppy urine to improve their complexions.

UGLINESS AND EVIL

The Tudors believed that beauty came from God, and that beauty and goodness were therefore the same thing. Tudor logic said that someone beautiful and clear-skinned was also a good person. The Tudors suspected people they considered ugly of being evil. Unattractive old women were accused of being witches and sometimes even burned alive. It was a high price to pay for having bad skin!

Unattractive women in Tudor England risked being accused of witchcraft. If found guilty, they could be executed.

THE RISE
-OF ROUGE-

After centuries when pale skin dominated fashion, colored cheeks became all the rage when Queen Elizabeth I of England started to color hers.

Out went pale and in came a healthy looking flush. Against her white complexion, the queen highlighted her cheeks with **rouge**. Rouge came in all kinds of shades of red, depending on what was added to the base. Little did they know it, but Elizabeth and those who followed her were slowly poisoning themselves through their skin.

A BIT OF COLOR

When rouge had been popular in ancient Greece, the Greeks had used natural red dyes. Crushed mulberries worked well, as did red beet juice or even strawberry juice. The Tudors took their rouge far more seriously. For the modern look, the brownish tone produced by red ochre was not quite right.

Elizabeth I covered her skin in a base of white lead, then added rouge to her cheeks to give them a healthy looking glow.

A DEADLY SHADE

The Tudors made brighter shades of rouge by adding substances to the white lead base of their makeup. The substances included madder and alkanet, made from plant roots, and cochineal, made by crushing dead beetles. The process had a high level of risk. The minerals mercuric sulfide and vermilion created a bright red tone, but were both poisonous—as was white lead itself. By the eighteenth century, men in **Georgian** England were just as likely to rouge their cheeks as women. If applying powder was too much trouble there was always prepared Spanish wool. This was a cloth infused with cochineal. It simply had to be moistened and then rubbed over the cheeks to give the desired color.

The cochineal dye was extracted by crushing thousands of tiny beetles.

to die for

People finally stopped using these kinds of rouge in the nineteenth century—but because they thought it was a sign of low **morals**, not because it caused slow poisoning and death. "Decent" women took to pinching their faces rather than using rouge to get a glow in their cheeks—and inadvertently saved their lives.

DYING FOR
- BEAUTY -

Georgian women used white lead, or ceruse, to cover up imperfections and provide a base for their makeup. Some paid with their lives.

The wealthier a woman, the more likely she was to poison herself with high-quality, lead-based cosmetics.

CERUSE

The most expensive ceruse had the highest lead content, but no one realized it. Even when women's eyebrows fell out, people did not make the connection with ceruse. One notable victim of ceruse was the Duchess of Coventry. The duchess and her sister, the Duchess of Hamilton, were celebrated beauties of Georgian London. Lady Coventry always painted her face—and was dead at the age of 28. Her sister wore less makeup, and outlived her by 30 years, although ceruse destroyed her looks. When ceruse damaged their complexions, women applied more ceruse to cover it up—making things worse.

The Duchess of Hamilton used so much ceruse that it eventually ruined her skin.

The side effects of ceruse included headaches, shortness of breath, cramps, dizziness, blindness—and early death. There were other risks, too. After years of applying red sandalwood, cochineal, brazilwood, and talc to her face, one woman's skin turned yellow.

Belladonna, from the deadly nightshade plant, produced eye drops that could cause blindness.

A HIGH PRICE

Round faces were popular, so women stuffed their cheeks with wax or cork balls known as "plumpers." A mouthful of plumpers made it difficult to speak, so some women went for the wide-eyed look instead. They added drops of belladonna ("beautiful lady") to their eyes to make their pupils look large and innocent. However, the toxic drops also caused blindness.

hello beautiful

Kitty Fisher (right) was one of the first celebrities who became famous mainly for being famous. Painters lined up to capture her beauty, and her clothes set fashions in London. In 1767, she died at age 28, just four months after her marriage. The likely cause of death was the effect of the lead-based cosmetics she always wore.

Chapter 4

THE NINETEENTH
- CENTURY -

*The nineteenth century was a tricky time for women. Any sign of **vanity** was frowned upon, but at the same time women were expected to look their best.*

Victoria came to the British throne in 1837 at just 18 years of age.

In 1789 the French revolted against their rulers. The king and many nobles lost their heads. It became a crime even to wear makeup, which was associated with the **nobility**. Following the French Revolution, France lost its place as the leader of European fashion.

ENGLAND RULES

In the 1830s, people looked to the young British queen, Victoria, for beauty trends. Her skin looked naturally fresh and clean, and everyone copied the style. Beauty manuals appeared, stressing the importance of exercise and fresh air to produce a healthy-looking complexion. Lead-based products were out, although some older women still wore a layer of white paint to hide their wrinkles. Victoria's influence helped save thousands of young women from putting poisonous creams on their faces.

THAT'S ROMANTIC

Not everyone wanted to look healthy, however. The early nineteenth century saw the rise of the Romantic movement, when poets and artists praised everything that was natural and wild. Those loved by Romantics such as the poet Lord Byron were fragile and innocent. They were meant to look as if they had never taken a walk or even been outdoors in the fresh air.

Lemon juice could help give an unhealthy look to the face—and a lemony smell!

The ideal Romantic heroine spent her time lying on the sofa looking pale and sick. To achieve this look, young women drank vinegar and rubbed lemon juice into their skin. To give them a look of wide-eyed innocence, they dropped belladonna into their eyes. The fact that it might cause blindness or even **paralysis** was not as important as looking the part.

The ultimate sickly figure: the Romantic poet Thomas Chatterton died at the age of just 17.

COVER
- UP -

Many Victorian women had little independence and little to do. With servants to take care of the house and children, many women stayed at home and concentrated on looking their best.

Wealthy women spent most of their time indoors, so the fashionable look was to have pale skin. Many women were careful to keep their skin this way.

STAYING PALE

When she went outdoors, a Victorian woman wore a bonnet and gloves and carried a parasol to keep the sun off her head. Indoors, she sat behind a **fire screen** to prevent the heat of the fire from making her face flushed. To achieve the palest possible skin without resorting to face paint, some women tried eating chalk, slate, or tea leaves. Daring beauties even tried a few drops of the metallic crystal **arsenic**. It was a deadly poison, so it was essential to take only a little!

The parlor was the heart of the Victorian family home—and where women spent most of their time.

KEEPING CLEAN

Like pale skin, another sign of wealth was taking frequent baths. The growing industrial cities were filthy, and those who could afford to work in offices or not to work at all wanted to look different from the poor who worked in dirty factories. The poor bathed infrequently, so they had terrible skin. They suffered from blackheads, which were believed to be "fleshworms" that crawled out of the skin. Magazines advertised all sorts of remedies for skin problems. One was a mixture of sulfur and cream to be applied at bedtime. The potion stank like rotten eggs, so there was no guarantee the wearer would be able to fall asleep!

A large bonnet, long sleeves, and gloves protect a fashionable young woman from the effects of the sun.

hello beautiful

The British **dandy** Beau Brummell loved taking baths. He spent three hours a day bathing and dressing before he was ready to go out. Brummell was considered the leader of fashion and was soon copied by powerful friends. His obsession with cleanliness spread. Bathing became fashionable and the British became cleaner.

MAKE IT
- YOURSELF -

Faced with the Victorian disapproval of cosmetics, many women followed those before them and made their own skin-care products using natural ingredients.

Beauty manuals rediscovered old recipes for skin lotions that used ingredients such as lemon, lavender, horseradish, sugar, and sour milk. At least women who raided the kitchen garden knew what they were putting on their faces.

CHEATED CUSTOMERS

The Victorian association of cosmetics with immoral behavior made women reluctant to be seen buying cosmetics. Instead, they relied on mail order. Immoral manufacturers laced their potions with poisons such as arsenic, white lead, and mercury.

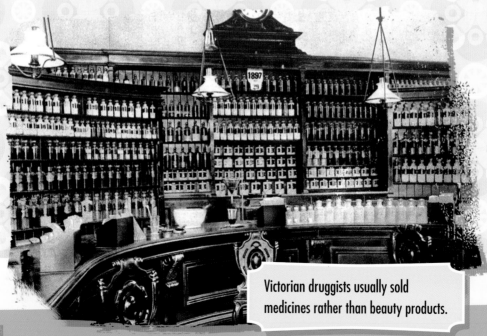

Victorian druggists usually sold medicines rather than beauty products.

IT MUST BE GOOD!

Some cosmetics sellers took advantage of women's reluctance to be seen buying in stores. Madame Rachel of Bond Street, London, advertised her products in the best women's journals. Her high prices and exclusive products attracted many wealthy society ladies. They wore heavy veils when they visited her salon in order to remain anonymous. Madame Rachel made great claims for her products, but most were fake. The healing water she claimed came from Jordan in the Middle East was ordinary London water. The "Magnetic Rock-Dew Water of Sahara for Removing Wrinkles" had never been near the Sahara Desert! As for Madame Rachel's "enamelling" face cream, it was simply deadly ceruse sold under another name.

The Jordan River was famous from Bible history, so its name helped sell "healing water" in London.

to die for

Common Victorian diseases such as smallpox left unsightly marks on victims' faces. It was considered acceptable to disguise such scars by covering them up. By the 1840s, every self-respecting drugstore in New York City had an in-house cosmetician. However, most of the cosmeticians' time was spent covering up the black eyes of male customers who had been fighting.

Skin care and cosmetics were big business in the twentieth century. Wearing makeup was no longer considered a sin.

Skin care entered a golden age as mass production made cheaper, safer creams and soaps available to everyone. In the 1920s, modern women threw caution to the wind and started to openly apply makeup.

ALL CHANGE

The end of the 1920s saw one of the biggest changes in the history of skin care. For centuries, the fashion had been for pale skin. Now, for the first time, darker tanned skins became fashionable. The arrival of wealthy American tourists on the French Riviera transformed the beauty business. In the summer of 1927, the fashion magazine *Vogue* put a tanned model on its cover. Tans were now a sign of wealth and leisure and became the look millions wanted to copy.

Palmolive advertised widely in magazines in the early twentieth century. The company made its first soap in 1898.

By the 1920s, "bathing beauties" showed off much more skin than in previous decades.

REGULATING THE BUSINESS

Another new development that shaped the look of beauty was the rise of Hollywood. Movie stars became the new fashion leaders, and millions of women wanted to copy the looks of their favorite stars. Skin care became big business—and attracted the attention of the government. In the United States, the 1906 Pure Food and Drug Act became the first step in protecting consumers by stamping out the many dangerous ingredients that were a staple of the skin-care business. For example, arsenic complexion wafers and radium bath salts became illegal. However, despite many attempts by federal agencies to regulate the skin-care market, many harmful products remained on sale. They included, for example, the hair-removal cream Koremlu, which contained rat poison. It was not until 1977 that the law required all ingredients to be listed on skin-care packaging.

BIG
- BUSINESS -

The arrival of the movies in the 1920s transformed skin care. The movie stars who loomed above audiences on the silver screen had to look their best.

For centuries, stage actors and actresses had used thick, oily makeup called greasepaint to make their skin appear normal in the bright lights of the stage. For close-ups in the movies, however, thick greasepaint looked terrible.

DO I REALLY LOOK LIKE THAT?

The man who solved the problem was Max Factor, a Polish immigrant who arrived in Los Angeles in 1904 to work in the new movie industry. In just 10 years, Max had perfected his own line of makeup powder for the movies. Soon Max Factor was not simply powdering the stars' faces. He was selling his makeup to millions of women in both the United States and Europe.

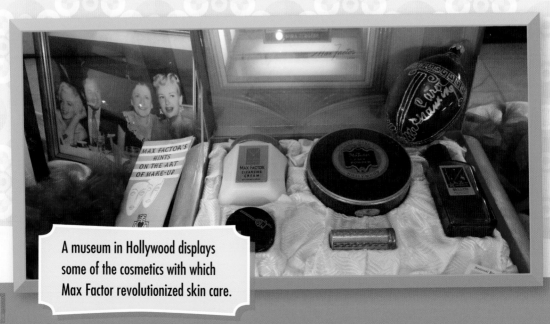

A museum in Hollywood displays some of the cosmetics with which Max Factor revolutionized skin care.

KEEP CLEAN

Screen makeup took its toll on the skin, but Hollywood stars tried to look as young and beautiful as possible. They used herbal **compresses** on their puffed-up eyes, rich creams on the backs of their hands, and eye drops to widen their pupils. Ordinary women copied not just the makeup the movie stars wore, but also the way they removed it. Women started to remove their makeup with Palmolive soap and Pond's cold cream, both of which boasted that they were good for the complexion. Most fashionable of all were new "beauty cream" lotions that were made in France and exported around the world.

A women's magazine from 1948 tells its readers the latest beauty tips.

hello beautiful

Max Factor's great breakthrough was to customize his cosmetics to suit each movie star's complexion and hair color. He made individual shades of makeup for stars such as Joan Crawford, Claudette Colbert, and Lena Horne. He also worked with male stars, such as Rudolph Valentino (movie poster, right), who got Max to make his skin look paler than it really was.

AFRICAN AMERICAN
- BEAUTY -

For much of history, there was little specialized skin care for African Americans. In the early 1900s, a few women set out to change that.

At the start of the twentieth century, many thought the ideal skin was clear, smooth—and pale. Where did that leave women of color?

NEW COMPANIES

To fill the gap, African American businesswomen such as Madam C. J. Walker and Annie Turnbo Malone started companies to sell cosmetics and hair products to black women. At the time, there was a fashion for products that **bleached** dark skin lighter, but Walker and Malone did not make such creams. They wanted customers to be proud of their skin tone. They advertised their products as being suitable for women who did manual work—as most African Americans did. There was a large potential market. There were nearly 10 million African Americans in the U.S. in 1910.

African American women at a town meeting in Florida in 1915.

OFF TO THE BEAUTY PARLOR

In 1916, another African Amerian woman, Nobia Franklin, opened a beauty salon in Fort Worth, Texas. Before long, she had a chain of stores and her own beauty school, trading under the name Madame N.A. Franklin. Although she started out selling hair products, like Walker and Malone, Franklin could see that African American women needed their own skin-care products. She created her own line, which included soap and face powder. They were created to flatter rather than whiten dark skin. The beauty school Franklin founded in Houston, Texas, is still in operation today. It is the oldest continuously operated beauty school in the United States.

These are some early hair products made by Madam C. J. Walker.

to die for

In the 1900s and 1910s, black Americans in the South were subject to **Jim Crow** laws. These laws restricted their rights. The fact that African American women created hair and skin-care products for other African Americans was revolutionary. It was even more remarkable that Madam C. J. Walker became one of the country's first self-made female millionaires.

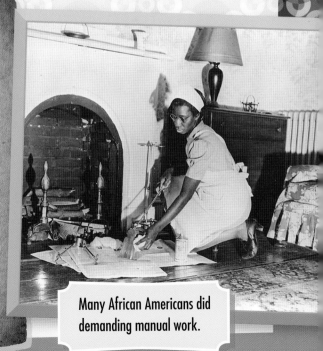

Many African Americans did demanding manual work.

CATCHING
- RAYS -

Until the 1920s, pale skin was a sign that someone lived a life of leisure. By the end of the decade, everyone wanted to look as if they spent their time lying in the sun.

The change came from the Industrial Revolution of the nineteenth century. In the past, workers had labored outdoors in the sun and their skin was dark. Now, however, factory workers rarely saw the sun, so their skin remained pale. Suddenly darker skin was a sign of wealth.

PALE NO MORE

The new fashion really took off in the 1920s. At the time, the French fashion designer Coco Chanel was probably the most fashionable woman in the world. Chanel took a cruise on the Mediterranean Sea, and her skin darkened from the sun. Photographs of her tanned face caused a storm. Now everyone wanted a tan. In the past, wealthy vacationers had avoided the sun. Now the rich and fashionable from all over Europe and the United States started to vacation on the beaches of the French Riviera.

Factory workers, like these women during World War I (1914–1918), were often unhealthily pale.

CATCHING RAYS

The fashion for a tan has lasted almost unbroken since the 1920s. This is partly because a suntan is a clear sign that someone is wealthy enough to take luxury vacations. Another contributing factor is that by the early twentieth century, doctors knew that exposure to the sun could be healthy (although too much unprotected exposure can cause skin cancer). Many Victorian children had suffered from a condition caused by rickets, which deforms the bones. Physicians learned that rickets was caused by a lack of vitamin D—which is provided by sunlight.

A woman in a backless bathing suit sunbathes in the 1950s.

hello beautiful

Many people thought of a suntan as a fashion accessory. However, protective sun creams weren't invented until 1938, so early sunbathers who overdid it felt the burn! It wasn't until 1978 that the Food and Drug Administration proposed regulating sunscreens and labeling them with their sun protection factor, or SPF.

GOING
- HOMEMADE -

In 1929, the *Great Depression* began in the *United States* and spread around the world. For most people, skin care became an unaffordable luxury.

As the economy slowed, millions of people lost their jobs. For most families, food and shelter took priority. Beauty treatments were a long way down the list.

GARDEN BEAUTY

Women who had access to a garden were lucky. They could use what they grew for skin care. Rose petals mixed with water made a refreshing face tonic and smelled good. Even the humble lettuce leaf revived and moisturized the face. Although eggs were expensive, Americans who kept hens could use a little egg white to make a face mask. It worked beautifully to tighten and tone the skin—plus it also meant they got to eat the yolk.

A jobless worker living in a tent during the Great Depression had little chance to take care of her skin.

A LITTLE TREAT

As the economy continued to shrink during the 1930s, people found it harder to make ends meet. Many goods became scarce or disappeared altogether. Still, many women were determined to keep some glamour in their lives. They continued with their homemade skin-care regimens. One simple tip from the time to keep skin free of wrinkles and lines was not to move the face—no smiling and definitely no laughing! People who did manage to laugh despite the gloom could use cold cream to keep their faces smooth. It was also useful for anything from cleaning the face to conditioning eyelashes.

Some people think egg whites can shrink pores, reducing oil and pimples.

to die for

Throughout history, people have made **poultices** to apply to the skin. One common poultice was a mixture of mustard powder and oil. It was used to treat conditions such as chest infections and also to stimulate the skin. The mustard gently warmed the skin—but if you accidentally used too much mustard, the skin burned!

Poultices are usually made from herbs and spices, such as mustard powder.

Chapter 6

THE TWENTY-FIRST
- CENTURY -

Skin care today combines high-tech and low-tech. Companies claim that their products are scientific, but they are also often natural and organic.

Eager to be taken seriously, the skin-care business has embraced all kinds of science. In the 1940s Elizabeth Arden introduced a face mask that used aluminum foil and microwaves to improve the skin. Today, laser treatment removes all kinds of skin imperfections.

SCIENTIFIC SKIN CARE

Most modern "scientific" ingredients in skin-care products are actually old. The alpha hydroxy acids (AHAs) that claim to stop the skin from aging are the same chemicals as in Cleopatra's bath of donkey milk.

Skin-care stores often use simple packaging to highlight the "natural" products inside.

One cosmetics company even dressed its sales assistants in department stores in white laboratory coats to underline its "scientific" approach. At the same time, companies boast that their products are "natural." For customers, it can all be a little confusing.

DO I LOOK YOUNG IN THIS?

At the start of the twenty-first century, people wanted to look as young as possible. Beauty companies marketed many skin-care products as being "anti-aging." They made extravagant claims for what were sometimes called "miracles in a pot." They often charged hundreds of dollars for tiny jars of cream.

In 2017, the mood started to shift. Women began to embrace their age rather than disguising it. To reflect the change, cosmetics companies began to drop their anti-aging labels and replace them with new "age-appropriate" products. Skin care was worth $121 billion in 2014, making it the most valuable sector of the beauty industry—so it pays for manufacturers to keep up with the latest beauty trends!

Many pop stars, such as Beyoncé, became icons for healthy and glowing skin in the early twenty-first century.

FACE
- TIME -

One trend of the last decade has been the rise of "me time" and indulging yourself at a spa. It's not just for women: men today are just as likely to go for a face treatment.

Since the time of the ancient Greeks and Romans, people have appreciated the benefits to one's health—and skin—of "taking the waters" at a spa. In many ways, skin care has come full circle.

TIME FOR ME

Today, spas are not just about mineral water but offer a whole range of body and face treatments. Spas vary widely, but the one thing they have in common is that they provide an opportunity to relax and rejuvenate. Having a beauty treatment, such as a facial, is now closely associated with a sense of all-around well-being and health. Although it is not really a medical procedure, it feels as if it is doing us a lot of good.

Spas offer many treatments, including face masks with slices of cucumber to refresh the eyes.

MEN'S GROOMING

Once again, the age of the dandy is back thanks to celebrities such as David Beckham and Sean Combs, who are happy to discuss their skin-care regimens. Men's grooming is now a multibillion-dollar business that shows no signs of slowing down. In 2013, men spent more on skin products than on shaving products for the first time. Just as male Romans sat in their steam baths to soften their skin, modern men often enjoy a facial tailored for their skin. As has been true throughout history, men and women today continue to appreciate that taking care of their skin is an essential part of feeling good.

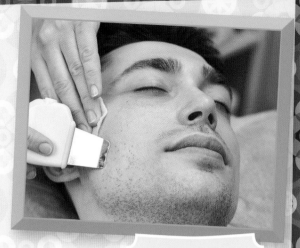

A man has a special treatment to remove stubble from his cheeks.

hello beautiful

Sean Combs, also known as P. Diddy or Puff Daddy, never goes to sleep without washing his face. He uses his favorite **serum** to keep his face looking good and has a passion for face masks. Combs' bathroom has so many skin-care products it looks like a home spa. He can try a different product every day if he wants to.

-TIMELINE-

c. 4000 BC Cosmetics are in widespread use in Sumer and ancient Egypt.

500s BC The ancient Greeks adopt a modest, natural-looking appearance for women.

69 BC Cleopatra is born in Egypt; she becomes famous for bathing in donkey's milk to soften her skin.

c. 0 The Roman writer Ovid recommends treating the skin with crocodile excrement.

AD 100s The physician and writer Galen invents the first recipe for cold cream.

AD 476 The Roman Empire is overthrown by Germanic peoples, and cosmetics largely disappear from Europe.

1095 The First Crusade begins as Christians fight Muslims for control of the Holy Land; Crusaders returning to Europe bring new cosmetics and other forms of skin care from Asia.

1100s Eleanor of Aquitaine becomes a leader of fashion in France and later in England.

1548 In Florence, Italy, Agnolo Firenzuola writes *On the Beauty of Women*, one of the first handbooks of beauty.

c. 1560 Queen Elizabeth I of England begins a fashion trend for using white face powder and rouge.

1767 Celebrated London beauty Kitty Fisher dies, probably from the harmful effects of lead-based makeup.

c. 1785 Beau Brummell becomes leader of the dandies in London.

1789	After the French Revolution, royalty and the nobility lose their role as leaders of fashion and cosmetics are outlawed.
1837	Victoria becomes queen of Britain. Despite being a noted beauty in her youth, she later turns against the use of cosmetics. Her example helps protect the skins of many young women.
1840s	Drugstores in the United States increasingly hire cosmeticians.
1898	Palmolive makes its first soap, based largely on palm oil and olive oil.
1904	Max Factor arrives in Los Angeles. Within 10 years he has built a business supplying makeup to movie stars.
1906	The Pure Food and Drug Act is a first attempt to control the ingredients of skin-care products.
1916	Nobia Franklin opens a beauty salon in Texas for African Americans.
1920s	Young American women openly wear makeup and have their hair cut short.
1927	Fashion magazine *Vogue* features a suntanned model on its cover for the first time.
1929	The Great Depression begins a period of low wages and high unemployment during which cosmetics are largely made at home.
1940s	Elizabeth Arden introduces an experimental face mask that uses aluminum foil and microwaves.
1977	U.S. law requires all ingredients to be listed on the packaging of skin-care products.
2013	For the first time, men spend more on male skin-care products than they do on shaving products.
2017	Cosmetics manufacturers launch what they describe as "age-specific" lines of cosmetics.

-GLOSSARY-

afterlife the place where people go when they are dead

alum a mineral-based compound used in dyeing and tanning

arsenic a poisonous metallic element

astringent causing the skin cells to tighten

bleached lightened the color of something

cold cream a cosmetic used to clean and soften the skin

complexion the natural color and texture of a person's face

compresses damp cloths applied to the skin to reduce swelling

cosmetics substances applied to the skin to improve its appearance

dandy a man who pays excessive attention to his appearance

exfoliators products that remove dead cells from the skin's outer layer

face mask a cosmetic that is spread on the face and left for some time

fire screen a portable screen placed in front of an open fire

gemstones precious or semiprecious stones used in jewelry

Georgian the period of British history from 1714 to 1840

Great Depression a period of economic slowdown in the 1930s, when many people had no work

hunter-gatherers early humans who hunted animals and gathered berries for food

immoral having low standards of behavior

Jim Crow the name for a series of laws that enforced racial segregation in the South

kohl a black powder widely used as eye makeup in the ancient world

leeches bloodsucking worms used in some medical treatments

minerals naturally occurring solids, such as crystals and salts

moisturizers cosmetics that prevent dryness in the skin

morals standards of behavior

mummies dried and preserved bodies of the dead

nobility the elite class of society

paralysis the condition of not being able to move

poultices soft, moist preparations applied to the skin

rejuvenate to make something look or feel younger

resin a sticky substance in tree bark

rosewater scented water made from rose petals and oils

rouge red powder or cream used to color the cheeks or lips

serum a usually lightweight, water-based substance that can be applied to the face, often to improve the look of the skin

translucent semitransparent

vain having too much pride in one's own appearance

vanity the quality of being vain

-FOR MORE INFORMATION-

BOOKS

Baum, Margaux, and Margaret Scott. *Fashion and Clothing*. New York, NY: Rosen Publishing, 2017.

Gourley, Catherine. *Flappers and the New American Woman: Perceptions of Women from 1918 Through the 1920s*. Minneapolis, MN: Twenty-First Century Books, 2008.

Higgins, Nadia. *Brilliant Beauty Inventions*. Minneapolis, MN: Lerner Publishing Group, 2014.

McKissack, Patricia and Frederick. *Madam C. J. Walker: Inventor and Millionaire*. Berkeley Heights, NJ: Enslow Publishers, 2013.

Webb, Sarah Powers. *Marie Antoinette: Fashionable Queen or Greedy Royal?* North Mankato, MN: Capstone Press, 2015.

WEBSITES

Ancient Egypt for Kids: Makeup
egypt.mrdonn.org/kohl.html
This Mr. Donn page gives more information about kohl.

Skin Facts
www.sciencekids.co.nz/sciencefacts/humanbody/skin.html
Read more about the body part that people have used all these bizarre methods on.

Taking Care of Your Skin
kidshealth.org/en/kids/skin-care.html?ref=search&WT.ac=msh-k-dtop-en-search-clk
This article has lots of information about caring for your skin.

-INDEX-